Who Moved My Faith?

Yvonne Little

ISBN: 979-8-9869188-0-8 (paperback)
979-8-9869188-1-5 (ebook)

Contents

Preface

"So," I can hear you saying, "you have written another book about faith. You have got to be kidding!"

If that's what you're thinking, then you're right. There is a lot written about faith already. Yet, in spite of that, Christians are still struggling with this subject which is the foundation of so many religions. Just ask any pastor and I'm sure he will agree his greatest challenge is getting his congregation to simply believe.

"OK, what's this book about?" you ask. "How is it any different to all the rest?"

When you get right down to it, the only difference will be, perhaps, my writing style and the revelation I received while writing. The Word does not change. It is always the same.

Let me say this, though. This book will not correct issues in your personal life which need to be corrected in order for faith to work. You will need to have taken "Saved 101" and have it pretty well down pat. The infilling of the "Holy Spirit 102" is also a prerequisite. With these foundations under your belt and a good church affiliation, you will be well on your way to locating your faith.

In this book, I will cover the experiences we face that require the use of faith. Yet, when most needed, our faith seems to often take flight. Instead of us moving mountains, the mountains move us. Thus, faith is missing in action. The examples in the Word, including the lessons Jesus taught, are more than just historical accounts. They are examples to show us how we too can obtain miracles and live in the supernatural blessings of God.

Most of us wait until our backs are against the wall, and then struggle to locate and understand faith. When we don't receive the miracle we need, God takes the blame. This is a gross error. Believers are to live, day by day, in the miraculous power of God, but the only way we can do this is by knowing how to operate in faith and bring to pass the manifestation of what we are believing Him for.

Jesus gave us the authority to use His name and speak these manifestations into existence in the natural realm. This book will cover instances and examples that Jesus demonstrated and shared with His disciples. Jesus clearly instructed them on how to locate and activate their faith. If you follow His example, then you will be able to activate your faith too.

Acknowledgments

I would like to thank Dr. Mark & Patti Virkler, of Christian Leadership University, for their commitment to educating the body of Christ and providing a spirit-filled environment in which to do so.

Much thanks to my instructor at CLU, Dr. Kusmich, for providing a learning environment that allowed me to find my place in the Kingdom of God. Dr. Kusmich, the freedom you gave permitted me to share my spiritual experiences and was instrumental in developing my call. You will never know how much that meant to me.

To Pastor D, Dennis Bordeaux, in Rochester, NY, thanks for assisting me in getting into Bible College. This one act of kindness completely changed my life. I am eternally grateful. Much love to you, your wife, and church family.

Last of all, to you, the reader, thank you for taking the time to read this book. I am blessed by your desire to read yet another book on faith. Like Paul:

> "I always pray to the God of our Lord Jesus Christ, the Father of glory, that He may grant you a spirit of wisdom and revelation [of insight into mysteries and secrets] in the [deep and intimate]

knowledge of him . . . [so that you can know and understand] what is the immeasurable and unlimited and surpassing greatness of His power in and for us who believe, as demonstrated in the working of His mighty strength."

(Ephesians 1:17, 19)

Dedication

This book is dedicated to my children—Danielle Ruffin, Albert Little, III and to my grandson, Jaden M. Ruffin, Jasmine Ruffin, Alena Little and Ashley Little

May the word dwell in your hearts and minds so that you may know and walk in the perfect will of God for your lives.

HONORING MY PARENTS:

Sebastian and Helen Fripp

Faith, Oh Faith, Where Art Thou?

It's Sunday morning and the church is packed. As usual, the pastor is excited, the congregation is standing on their feet, and you can hear the shouts of joy and echoes of "I am more than a conqueror, and I will not be defeated!"

You realize you are in a war, but you're not sure of the directions to the battlefield or how to use your weapon—you just know you have a weapon and you better be using it. You are standing in faith for a particular thing, yet it has not manifested. Now you find yourself thinking, *'Am I in faith?'*

Perhaps you are new to the faith, or maybe, like many of us, you have been around the subject of faith for so long that you have gray hairs. Either way, you are continuing to grow and learn each day.

Jesus spent a lot of time discussing faith with the disciples. Obviously, it was very important to him. He even rebuked them for not demonstrating, or outwardly showing, that they had any faith at all.

Let's use this example: You invite me over for dinner, but you live many miles away. It's a long drive to your home, and upon arriving I realize I need to use the restroom.

As I walk through your door, you greet me, take my coat, and ask if I would like a refreshment. I say, "Yes, thank you," and then ask, "Where is the bathroom?"

Notice I did not ask if there *was* a bathroom in the house. Why? Because I already knew there would be one in your home.

So, in the same way, when Jesus asked the disciples, "Where is your faith?" that obviously must mean they did have faith—even if it wasn't apparent at that time!

> "And he said unto them, Why are ye so fearful? How is it that ye have no faith?"
>
> (MARK 4:40 KJV)

What do you mean you don't have a bathroom? Everybody has a bathroom (at least in the free world), and in the same way, everybody has faith!

Jesus was making reference to the faith the disciples already had but were just not utilizing. Do you get it? How could the disciples walk with Jesus every day, be publicly rebuked about their lack and knowledge of faith, and not feel at some point like they had completely lost contact with it?

If you have ever felt the same way, know that you are not alone. Trust me, we have ALL been there.

This book is designed to help you locate your faith and overcome the obstacles, fear and trembling we all face when we are believing God for what WE think is impossible.

A major point Jesus makes is that no faith equals fear.

In Matthew 8:25:

> "And his disciples came to him, and awoke him, saying, Lord save us: we perish."
>
> (KJV)

Before we go further, let's examine the situation:

- Were they in a ship at sea? *Yes.*
- Were they in the middle of a storm? *Yes.*
- Was the ship covered with waves? *Yes.*

This was a very real and serious situation. The circumstances indicate that their ship was about to sink with them on board.

> "He [Jesus] replied, 'You of little faith, why are you so afraid? Then he got up and rebuked the winds and the waves, and it was completely calm."
>
> (MATTHEW 8:26 NIV)

> "And he said unto them, Where is your faith? And they being afraid wondered, saying one to another, What manner of man is this! For he commandeth even the winds and water, and they obey him."
>
> (LUKE 8:25 KJV)

"Where is your faith?" Jesus asked the disciples.

Recently, a girlfriend called and asked if I could meet with her immediately. She was very upset, so we arranged to meet for tea at Barnes & Noble.

Soon after, we were sitting together sipping Chai tea, one of our favorites, and she began to explain what had happened. I was shocked to learn my friend was heartbroken because her fiancé had called off their engagement.

As we sat there in the bookstore, I did all I could to encourage her and let her know that life would go on. "It's his loss," I said. "You're so beautiful, and so attractive, that I know it won't be long before you find the real man of your dreams."

She straightened her shoulders, resolutely twisted her neck, and gave me a high-five in agreement to everything I had said.

Then, with that taken care of, I said, "Now let's get some food, girl. I'm hungry."

Immediately, she curled her shoulders inward and her countenance changed to sorrow. She slowly leaned back in the comfortable chair, and said, "I'm sorry. You go ahead and order, girl. I can't eat."

I realized that although, in her heart, she agreed with everything I had said, and would be able to stand strong and get on with her life, the pain she was feeling at that moment was very real, and those circumstances were affecting her appetite.

What's my point? Simply that emotions are real. Circumstances and situations will arise, sometimes very unexpectedly, but just because you FEEL like the world is coming to an end, doesn't mean it is. The fact that my friend was not FEELING like eating as she waited for her strength to return, is OK—and that's what I let her know as I continued to comfort her. But I ate.

But back to Jesus and the disciples on the boat....

You may be saying to yourself by now, 'Why spend so much time on one incident in the Bible?' I challenge you to meditate on these scriptures and pray and ask the Lord to open your spiritual eyes to what is happening and the message the Holy Spirit is teaching us here.

Can you just imagine the scene in the boat that day? These guys had been out on a boat a multitude of times before—probably since childhood, for some. I would almost be willing to guarantee that this was not the first storm they had ever encountered, but it appears to be the first storm where they lost control of the situation—at least, so they thought.

In Mark 4:35–38, we read:

> "On that same day [when] evening had come, He said to them, Let us go over to the other side [of the lake] . . . And a furious storm of wind [of hurricane proportions] arose, and the waves kept beating into the boat, so that it was already becoming filled. But He [Himself] was in the stern [of the boat], asleep on the [leather] cushion; and they awoke Him and said to Him, Master, do You not care that we are perishing?"

From Matthew's account of the same event:

> "And after He got into the boat, His disciples followed Him. And suddenly, behold, there arose a violent storm on the sea, so that the boat was being covered up by the waves; but He was sleeping. And they went and awakened Him saying, Lord, rescue and preserve us! We are perishing! And He said to them, Why are you timid and afraid, O you of little faith? Then He got up and rebuked the winds and the sea, and there was a great and wonderful calm (a perfect peaceableness)."
>
> (MATTHEW 8:23-26.)

Notice in Mark's version, it says that the waves were "beating into the boat, so that it was already becoming filled." Also, before that, note in verse 35 that it was Jesus who had said to the disciples, "Let us go over to the other side of the lake."

So get this—the disciples are hanging out with Jesus. Suddenly He says, "Get in the boat. We are going to the other side of the lake."

They got the bit about getting into the boat but somehow must have missed the second part. When Jesus entered the boat, His intention was for all of them to go to the other side of the lake, just like He said. But now the waves are violently beating against the boat, and overflowing into it so that it's close to sinking. The disciples are petrified.

Have you ever been in a situation like that? Don't answer—
we probably all have at some time or other. Life is going along
just fine, and you're praising and thanking the Lord. Jesus is
Lord of your life, and you are singing, dancing and thanking
God for another day. Then suddenly a situation occurs....

Anyway, back to the boat. The disciples rush to Jesus for
help. Now, rushing to Jesus for help was not the problem;
it was the *way* they went to Him. They ran screaming and
shouting the circumstances, and describing their apparent
fall and impending demise—all the while, in a state of
heightened fear. Code: RED!

Have you ever been suddenly startled out of a deep sleep?
Well, that's what the disciples did to Jesus. Not only did they
go in fear over the circumstances, they began accusing Him
of not caring.

Suppose they had gone to Jesus in faith instead, and reminded
him of the miracles they had seen so far. Or remembered
how He had taught them things they would have never
been able to comprehend from any other teacher. Imagine if
Jesus had awoken to the sound of THEM—the disciples—
shouting at the wind and sea to be still, instead of shouting
the circumstances at Him. You may want to meditate on that
thought for a minute before moving on to Chapter Two....

Faith-Faith-Faith-Faith-Faith

Jesus said it was our faith that would remove mountains. So, get ready—here come the mountains.

Knowing Jesus and the Word, like I do, I know He made that statement for a reason. When facing a mountain, Christians often make the mistake of thinking that must mean they have no faith. However, Jesus did not say if you have faith there will never be a mountain. He said if you have faith, it (your faith) would remove the mountain.

"Well, how do I do that?" you ask.

First, don't do what the disciples did. Contrary to what your grandma said, don't go to Jesus telling him about all your troubles. He already knows. He knew before you asked for an audience with him. He knew before you got into that situation. He knows all things.

I hate to be the one to tell you, but Jesus is not impressed with tears and sobbing, or you getting yourself all tied up in a knot of anguish and begging Him for help. Ask the disciples.

Let's see, from the Word of God, what impressed Jesus.

Matthew 8:5-10, 13:

> "When Jesus had entered Capernaum, a centurion came to him, asking for help. 'Lord,' he said, 'my servant lies at home paralyzed and in terrible suffering.'
>
> Jesus said to him, 'I will go and heal him.'
>
> The centurion replied, 'Lord, I do not deserve to have you come under my roof. But just **say the word**, and my servant will be healed. For I myself am a man under authority, with soldiers under me. I tell this one, 'Go' and he goes; and that one, 'Come,' and he comes. I say to my servant, 'Do this,' and he does it.'
>
> When Jesus heard this, he was <u>astonished</u> and said to those following him, 'I tell you the truth, I have not found anyone in Israel with such <u>great faith</u>.'

Then Jesus said to the centurion, 'Go! It will
be done just as you believed it would.' And his
servant was healed at that very hour."

(NIV)

Many of you will know the story of the centurion whose
servant was sick and in pain. Jesus said, "I will come and
heal him."

But, what did the centurion say? If I may paraphrase, he said,
"Oh no, that won't be necessary." He gave honor to Jesus'
position and abilities. He said, "I know about you. You are
awesome. And based on what I know about you, all you have
to do is speak like you always do and that boy's situation is
going to change!"

In verse 10, Jesus' comments to the centurion are a whole lot
different to his comments to the disciples back on the boat.
Jesus was blown away by the man's statements. The Bible
says that He started speaking to the crowd, those that had
followed him, about this man's faith.

In verse 13, Jesus tells the man to go with the knowledge that
as he has believed, so it will be done unto him. The servant
was healed that same hour.

For me, this is one of the most powerful stories in the written
word. The centurion was able to get a revelation of who Jesus

was based on authority alone and how authority works. He clearly explains this to us in the scripture.

Historically, the centurion was a professional officer in the Roman Army—a commander. Most centurions commanded about a century (centuria) of eighty men. This man, not being a Jew, understood authority and that understanding got him a miracle from Jesus.

Unfortunately, in our society today, people do not respect and understand authority. People don't respect the President of the United States. However, this attitude is not only in America. Look at the world news and it's easy to see there is little respect for authority. Demonstrations in the streets, violence in the workplace and schools are clear indications of a lack of respect for authority. It's not just respect for the people in authority; we must also respect their positions of authority, as well.

The centurion received public mention from Jesus regarding his faith, while the disciples—men chosen and handpicked by Him for ministry—were rebuked for not demonstrating the same faith; faith they already had.

Now, you know, they had to feel a little stupid right at that moment, and perhaps even a little envious. Here they are walking, talking, eating and fellowshipping with Jesus, and this guy comes out of nowhere and, just like that, gets a miracle and the attention of Jesus. Why? Because of his faith which he demonstrated.

At this point, you might want to go back to Chapters One and Two and reread the two different accounts of how these men came to Jesus, what their attitude was like and what they said that got Jesus' attention. Also, notice the different reactions from Jesus.

In Mark Chapter 11, Jesus addresses the mountain-moving faith I mentioned earlier. Let's start with verse 11:

> "He went out to Bethany together with the Twelve [apostles]. On the day following, when they had come away from Bethany, He was hungry. And seeing in the distance a fig tree [covered] with leaves, He went to see if He could find any [fruit] on it [for in the fig tree the fruit appears at the same time as the leaves]. But when He came up to it, He found nothing but leaves, for the fig season had not yet come.
>
> And He said to it, No one ever again shall eat fruit from you. And His disciples were listening [to what He said]."
>
> (MARK 11:11-14.)

John 11:18 tells us that "Bethany was near Jerusalem, only about two miles away."

Jesus is traveling from Bethany to Jerusalem and becomes hungry. Seeing no figs on a fig tree, He begins to talk to the tree, and then curse it.

I often wonder what the disciples must have been thinking. They heard Him speak to the tree, but said nothing. I find this so strange. I don't know about you, but if I'm hanging out with you in the park and you start speaking to a tree, I'm going to ask you what the heck you are doing!!! But the disciples kept their silence and said nothing. Perhaps, they were afraid they would say the wrong thing like on the boat. Keep in mind, no one saw anything different about the tree after Jesus spoke to it.

Jesus and the disciples go into Bethany, where He preaches in the temple and drives out the moneychangers. He turns over the tables and completely shuts down business in the market for the day. Today, this would be equivalent to shutting down Wall Street or the Federal Reserve Bank. It was HUGE! When all the drama is over, Jesus begins to teach the people about the written word. Again, I'm wondering, what the disciples were thinking. Are you? Some day in the ministry with Jesus, huh?

Mark 11, verse 19 tells us that in the evening He and the disciples left the city.

Verses 20-21:

> "In the morning, when they were passing along, they noticed that the fig tree was withered [completely] away to its roots. And Peter **remembered** and said to Him, Master, look! The fig tree which You doomed has withered away!"

At this point, I would like to reiterate that Jesus was on His way from Bethany to Jerusalem when he saw a fig tree. He went up to it to get something to eat. However, upon not finding any figs, He speaks to the tree and says that no one will ever eat of the tree again.

Now the disciples heard this. Yet, according to the Bible, they did not say anything about it at all. Neither did they notice anything different about the tree. However, when passing the same tree the next day, Peter notices the tree is withered and dried up from the roots. Only then does Peter say something about the tree. He says, "Master, look at the tree which You cursed." (In other words, the tree WE HEARD YOU SPEAK TO yesterday.) "Something has happened to it. You told that tree to be cursed, and it is cursed."

Notice, Jesus did not pat Himself on the back. Instead, He immediately began to teach the disciples about faith. In verses 23-24, He said:

> "Truly I tell you, whoever says to this mountain, Be lifted up and thrown into the sea! and does not doubt at all in his heart but believes that what he says will take place, it will be done for him. For this reason I am telling you, whatever you ask for in prayer, believe (trust and be confident) that it is granted to you, and you will [get it]."

Again, notice that believing is directly connected to your mouth—not your emotions, not your tears, not your hope, not your wishing. IT IS IN YOUR SAYING!

Jesus taught the disciples a very important lesson here regarding faith. He told them that saying and believing are directly related. If you believe, you will say; if you say, you will believe. You must believe that what you are saying will come to pass.

Jesus never looked back at the tree and said, "Gee I sure hope that tree withers like I told it to." Or when leaving Jerusalem, said, "I need to go see IF that tree withered like I told it to do." He knew once He spoke to that tree it was a done deal.

What is it you must speak to? What tree in your life needs to wither from the root? Jesus set the example and showed us how to take authority over situations and get the results we desire. Just like the centurion said, we must speak the Word only because we are in authority.

What in the World are You Talking About?

In today's society, communication is at an all time high. With the advent of such things as the desktop computer, laptop, cable TV, cell phones, and PDA's, we are constantly connected and communicating with each other. We are a society of information, information, information. Yet, the body of Christ is still battling sickness, disease and many other struggles—all of which Christ came to redeem us from.

Not long ago, I was traveling down the highway and noticed a billboard sign. The sign was advertising miracles. "We are the place where miracles happen," it said. That's what made me notice the sign in the first place. However, the miracles were not being advertised by the local church. They were being advertised by the local hospital.

Now don't get upset and get me wrong. Hospitals and doctors are wonderful. I thank God every day for that profession and for the qualified people who work and function in the medical field. Yet, when was the last time you laid hands on someone and told them to be healed in the name of Jesus? When was the last time you went up to a hospital ward and said, "In the name of Jesus, everybody out of here now. Be healed; go home"?

Most local churches advertise: "Come to our church. We're family oriented!" A family oriented church is wonderful! Every church should be family oriented, but what if the local church took out a one page ad that said, "Come see what Jesus is like this Sunday morning. Make sure you bring somebody blind, or crippled, or just acting crazy." That's modern language for demon possessed.

Jesus said, "and these signs shall follow them that believe." I want you to see, again, what Jesus said about your faith. In Mark 16:14 it says:

> "Afterward He appeared to the Eleven [apostles themselves] as they reclined at table; and He reproved and reproached them for their unbelief (their lack of faith) and their hardness of heart, because they had refused to believe those who had seen Him and looked at Him attentively after He had risen [from death]."

Jesus appears to the disciples, and he again has to rebuke them for their hardness of heart and unbelief. No doubt, they felt like they had misplaced their faith—the same faith

Jesus keeps referring to and that they are having such a hard time grasping its concept. In my imagination, I can see them now, thinking... "Here he goes again."

Even after rising from the dead, Jesus is still teaching and instructing the disciples on the subject of faith. Obviously, this is an important subject!

So don't be so hard on yourself. Just as Jesus was patient with the disciples, so is He patient with us. Just as He taught them, He wants to teach you. That is why He sent the Holy Spirit. He knew we would need a teacher.

Verse 17: "And these signs shall follow the PREACHERS, EVANGELISTS, APOSTLES...."

NO, NO, NO! Jesus says these signs shall follow them— that's you, me, and us—that believe.

So what are the signs that will follow to let the world know you have faith? In Jesus' name, YOU shall cast out devils, and YOU shall speak with new tongues. Please note: these are the two things Jesus mentions first, so they are obviously important to Him. Casting out demons and speaking with new tongues.

Surely, by now you are saying, "What in the world are you talking about?" I'm talking about the specific instructions that Jesus left to the body of Christ; the instructions that hardly anyone seems to be talking about. Jesus has said that if YOU have faith, then you will be doing these things.

Verse 18:

> "They will pick up serpents; and [even] if they drink anything deadly, it will not hurt them; they will lay their hands on the sick, and they will get well."

WOW! What a statement. This makes us as good as Jesus was when He was on the earth.

Verse 20:

> "And they went out and preached everywhere, while the Lord kept working with them and confirming the message by the attesting signs and miracles that closely accompanied [it]. Amen (so be it)."

After all that rebuke and teaching, the disciples finally got it. The only thing that caused them to overcome was obedience to what Jesus said to do.

Today, many Christians reject the idea of being filled with the Spirit and speaking in tongues. Oh, and let's not talk about demons. Well, that is just what Satan wants. Let's not talk about him, and as long as we don't, God can get the blame for all the bad things happening to everybody.

But, let's get back to faith. So, as we've seen, there are two important things that Jesus said will let Him know if you are operating in faith:

1. What you say; and
2. The signs, or lack thereof, that follow you.

It is important that every believer spend time in prayer, asking the Holy Spirit to reveal Himself to them in this area. The Body of Christ is lacking in the area of a demonstration of faith. We must overcome this individually, as well as corporately, in order that the world may see Christ in and through us.

Jesus' ministry did not end when He left the earth. His ministry is to continue in and through the local body. Every believer has a role to play. Every believer has a responsible position that is equally as important as the pastor, the bishop or the evangelists. We must study the Word and develop our faith in order to become the overcomers Jesus intended for us to be.

Oh, My God!

"You mean I have to actually do something to demonstrate to God that I have faith?"

Absolutely!

"Oh, my God!"

Calm down. It's going to be OK. Just like the disciples finally got it, so will you.

First, if you believe the Bible, you will certainly need to be filled with the Holy Spirit, with the evidence of speaking in tongues. There are many books you can get to help you. Get a hold of your pastor. If your church doesn't practice this, find one that does. I'm not telling you to leave your church, but I am encouraging you to find someone who can minister to you in this area.

Sick people are everywhere, so I don't think you will have too much trouble in that area. And demons, let's not even go there. Now, don't go to work tomorrow and start screaming at your boss for the devil to come out of him or her. If you do, you will probably need to use your new found faith to find a job. Just hold tight.

Hook up with a good local church and get involved. Trust me, local churches need YOU and will be glad to have you involved in the ministry of helps.

Many churches today have Bible or leadership schools. Check online Bible schools. Remember, the disciples were taught and trained by Jesus before He turned them loose on society.

"You mean I have to study the Bible?"

Absolutely!

"Oh, my God!"

Calm down. It's going to be OK. The Bible is a book, and once you are filled with the

Holy Spirit, you will read it with clear understanding. Again, you will need to find a ministry that is interested in helping you grow in Christ and becoming knowledgeable in the things pertaining to the Word. That is the only way you will grow and develop this thing we call faith—STUDY, STUDY, STUDY.

Think about how much time you have spent during your lifetime to learn all you know up until this point. Now, suppose you had been able to spend an equal amount of time learning the Word of God. Just think what a spiritual giant you would be today. Well, it's not too late. The only thing required is for you to invest the time. Ask any successful person how they achieved their level of success and they will tell you they invested time in their goal and dreams.

Jesus has given each of us the success manual. All we have to do is read and do what it says.

Oh My God!

The book of Ezra tells us that King Artaxerxes resumed his favor upon the Jews. Ezra 7:1–10:

> "After these things, during the reign of Artaxerxes king of Persia, Ezra son of Seraiah, the son of Azariah, the son of Hilkiah, the son of Shallum, the son of Zadok, the son of Ahitub . . . this Ezra came up from Babylon. He was a teacher **well versed in the Law of Moses**, which the LORD, the God of Israel, had given. The king had granted him everything he asked, for the hand of the LORD his God was on him. . . . For Ezra had devoted himself to the study and observance of the Law of the LORD, and to teaching its decrees and laws to Israel."
>
> (NIV)

Notice, the Word says Ezra devoted HIMSELF to the study and observance of the Law of the Lord. Also, notice the king granted him EVERYTHING he asked for because the hand of the Lord was on him.

Let's look at 2 Timothy, chapter 2, verse 15:

> "Study to shew thyself approved unto God, a workman that needeth not to be ashamed, rightly dividing the word of truth."
>
> (KJV)

It's interesting that although people like others to know how much scripture they know, the Word says we are to demonstrate to God that we have knowledge of it.

In the book of Daniel, chapter 1, verse 4, King Nebuchadnezzar requested youths who were "skillful in all wisdom, discernment and understanding, apt in learning knowledge, competent to stand and serve in the king's palace." These youths were also to be taught literature and the language of the Chaldeans.

In verse 17:

"As for these four youths [Daniel, Shadrach, Meshach and Abednego], God gave them knowledge and skill in all learning and wisdom, and Daniel had understanding in all [kinds of] visions and dreams."

In addition to the skills they already had, God gave these four young men something extra. I don't know about you, but as I study the Word each day, I pray for an extra special anointing; an extra special blessing. If He did this for the Hebrew boys, He can do it for you and me.

If Jesus showed up at your house this evening for dinner, I'm sure you would prepare a wonderful meal. You might even call a caterer. I mean, after all, Jesus is coming to dinner. You may even call your friends and family to tell them the good news.

Dinner is finished and you settle back in your chairs. Jesus says, "Now, you know My Word and I are one, so let's discuss My Word."

What would your reaction be? What would you say? Would you have as much to say as Jesus? Remember, He left His complete Word with us here on earth.

What You Say!

If you just broke out in a cold sweat reading Chapter Five, wipe your brow. You will be fine. That's what this book is designed to help you learn—how to speak the Word and get results, regardless of the circumstances.

Remember when you prepared for your driver's license test? You were given a little book explaining the rules of the road, so you would have everything you need to be successful in answering a series of questions in the driving knowledge test. Upon answering those questions accurately, and passing the driving test, you would then receive a driver's license. Well, the Word of God is sort of like that.

The Bible is a book that explains what is required in order for you to be successful in life. Upon study of the book, and putting it into practice, you will receive the manifestation of the abundant life Jesus promised.

There will be tests—trust me. However, just like that little booklet gave you assistance in learning to drive, so too does the Word of God give you confidence for life. There are many other books, founded on God's Word, that are designed to assist. I implore you to seek these out and add them to your bookshelf.

Remember when Jesus was talking to the disciples and telling them they could have what they say? Well, that same principle applies to you—in both a positive and negative sense.

"What?" you say.

Yes, that's exactly right.

I know no one likes talking about death, but do you realize that every time you talk contrary to the Bible, you are talking death?

Do you realize that every time you talk contrary to the Bible, you are talking death?

"Oh no!"

Oh yes! Get your Bible, find a comfortable chair and let's take a look together. Proverbs 18:21:

> "Words kill, words give life; they're either poison or fruit—you choose."
>
> (THE MESSAGE)

Notice, words can give life, or they can kill—the choice is yours. If you comprehend nothing else in this book, *please* understand this one thing. Today, yesterday and your whole future are tied to your words. That is exactly the point Jesus was trying to get over to the disciples. You must find out what the Bible wants you to speak, and then *say it*! Not once or twice and then give up because you don't see immediate change. No, keep saying it until you *do* see change.

Now imagine that every time you say a word contrary to your healing, or contrary to the long and healthy life promised to you in the covenant, you are actually cutting your lifespan short.

I'm not saying you are never going to die, but why die before you have lived a long, healthy and prosperous life here on earth? The important thing to remember is every time you allow someone to convince you that the promises of God are not true, you let them move your faith. So, my question to you is: "Who moved your faith?" Have you ever thought that, perhaps, it was YOU alone?

Let's identify a few faith movers:

- Lack of finances;
- Sickness;
- Spiritually disconnected from God—not born again;

- Loneliness;
- Depression;
- Pressure;
- Vices (e.g. drugs, alcohol abuse, etc.);

I have left space for you to add your own personal faith movers.

Reading through this list, you would think it was a description of the world, but unfortunately, it is also a picture of most of the body of Christ. Thankfully, this is getting ready to change. Praise the Lord.

Let's look at some faith-movers in scripture:

Numbers 13:1–2:

> "And the Lord said to Moses, Send men to explore and scout out [for yourselves] the land of Canaan, which I give to the Israelites. From each tribe of their fathers you shall send a man, every one a leader or head...."

Notice, God speaks to Moses about land He says He has already given the Israelites. I suggest you read the entire book of Numbers to get the complete picture of what is happening.

The children of Israel have left the bondage of Egypt, had the miracle of crossing the Red Sea, and now God wants to take them into the Promised Land. The spies go out as ordered and come back with the report of what they have seen.

Numbers 13:27-28:

> "They told Moses, We came to the land to which you sent us; surely it flows with milk and honey. This is its fruit. But the people who dwell there are strong, and the cities are fortified and very large; moreover, there we saw the sons of Anak [of great stature and courage]."

This report, these words, get the people stirred up and upset.

Notice carefully what happens in verse 30:

> "Caleb quieted the people before Moses, and SAID, Let us go up at once and possess it; we are well able to conquer it."

This is Caleb's confession of faith.

Verse 31:

> "But his fellow scouts said, We are not able to go up against the people [of Canaan], for they are stronger than we are."

Then verse 33 is where they really sealed their fate:

> "There we saw the Nephilim [or giants], the sons of Anak, who come from the giants; and we were in our own sight as grasshoppers, and so we were in their sight."

Chapter 14 says they cried and wept all night. Then a fight almost broke out against Moses. This is what a bad confession will do.

The people chose not to believe what God said. They chose not to believe what Caleb said and, as a result, never entered the land God promised and prepared for them.

2 Kings 16 tells of Asa, King over Judah, who was extremely rebellious against the Lord and His commandments, even though the Lord had given Asa many victories. The Lord sent Hanani the seer to Asa to state the wrath of God for his rebellion. Asa has the seer put in prison and begins to oppress the people of God.

What has always been interesting to me is that Asa became ill with a disease in his feet. The Bible says the disease became very severe. Even so, Asa did not seek the Lord but relied on the physicians. He subsequently died, and his son, Jehoshaphat, reigned over Judah in Asa's stead.

Disobedience is a major faith-mover. It causes one to lose focus and operate in poor judgment and poor decision making.

Luke 18:18-30. The rich young ruler allowed the thought of being separated from his possessions to move his faith.

Matthew 26: 74. Peter allowed the circumstances surrounding Jesus' arrest to move his faith, resulting in him denying he ever knew Jesus.

Now let's identify the solutions from the Word of God:

- Know what the Word of God says about your situation;
- Act the Word according to scripture;
- Say the end result (prayer, speaking);
- See (imagine) the end result; and
- Give God glory for the victory (praise, thanksgiving, worship).

We'll look at these faith-moving solutions in more detail in the next chapters.

Know the Word of God and What it Says

The importance of study of the Bible has already been discussed in Chapter Four.

Jesus himself was a student of the Word. Let's look at Luke 4:16:

> "He [Jesus] went to Nazareth, where he had been brought up, and on the Sabbath day he went into the synagogue, as was his custom."
>
> (NIV)

As we can see, going to the synagogue was a habit for Jesus. It was something He did on a regular basis. The synagogue was a meeting place. There were many of them.

Continuing on, in verse 16b-17:

> "And he stood up to read. The scroll of the prophet Isaiah was handed to him. Unrolling it, he found the place where it is written..."
>
> (NIV)

Let's look at something important. Jesus was a church-goer—a church-goer who could read. I want to bring this up-to-date so you can relate to what is going on. Just imagine if Jesus had stood up in the synagogue and stumbled over the words he was reading. Or worse, when they handed Him the scroll, He had asked, "What's this?" Reading is a very basic, yet necessary, ability we all must develop in the Kingdom. Our ability to read and study is crucial. If someone tells me they do not like to read, I feel they either can't or simply lack wisdom. Either situation can easily be corrected.

In the following section we will cover a lot of scripture. Take your time and pause to review if you feel the need to.

Luke 4:1-13. The devil confronted and challenged Jesus. Verse 2 says Jesus "was tempted (tried, tested exceedingly) by the devil."

Verses 3–4:

> "Then the devil said to Him, If You are the Son of God, order this stone to turn into a loaf [of bread].

> And Jesus replied to him, It is written, Man shall
> not live and be sustained by (on) bread alone but
> by every word and expression of God."

Jesus did not pick up a rock and throw it at the devil. Nor did He pull out a sword and attempt to have a physical battle. Instead, He opened His mouth and began to speak the written Word.

Verses 5-8:

> "Then the devil took Him up to a high
> mountain and showed Him all the kingdoms
> of the habitable world in a moment of time [in
> the twinkling of an eye]. And he said to Him, To
> You I will give all this power and authority and
> their glory (all their magnificence, excellence,
> preeminence, dignity, and grace), for it has been
> turned over to me, and I give it to whomever I
> will. Therefore if You will do homage to and
> worship me [just once], it shall all be Yours.
>
> And Jesus replied to him, Get behind Me,
> Satan! It is written, You shall do homage to and
> worship the Lord your God, and Him only shall
> you serve."

If you continue reading this passage of scripture, you will see that the devil finally left Jesus. But suppose Jesus had been unprepared for the attack of the enemy? Suppose He didn't know the scriptures and had no answer for him? This is another reason why it is so important for believers to study and build themselves up with the Word of God.

The scripture states Jesus was full of the Holy Spirit and had been praying and fasting for forty days, and still the enemy attempted to attack. So know that you can be doing everything right and the enemy will still launch an attack. But, just like Jesus, we must be prepared with the Sword of the Spirit—the Word of God. Jesus was not moved by what the enemy had to say. Jesus had more to say than the devil. What the devil said was a lie; what Jesus said was the truth.

If you read further in this same passage, you will reach the place where Jesus goes into the synagogue and begins to teach from the book of Isaiah (Luke 4:16-21). Again, the Bible is letting us know that Jesus knew the scriptures.

The Bible is God Himself speaking to you. If you cannot, or do not, read the Bible, how will you know what God is saying? Today, the Bible is available on CD, and that's a great place to start. Even so, we all must learn to read, meditate and study the Word.

There are other types of reading material as well. Investing in good books, CDs and DVDs is a way of investing in yourself and gaining knowledge.

If you are a parent, begin teaching and training your children the importance of developing good reading habits now. This will stay with them throughout their lifetime.

Returning to Luke 4, notice in verse 17 that Jesus began to read from the book of Isaiah. In verse 21 He goes on to say, "Today this scripture has been fulfilled while you are present and hearing."

Jesus already knew the passage of scripture from Isaiah because he was a student of the Word. You must know the Word if you are going to live the victorious life.

Tradition has portrayed Jesus as a man who woke up one morning, collided with a dove that just happened to fall from the sky, and then went out and started preaching to people. This is so wrong. Jesus had a plan. He fulfilled the plan of redemption that delivered mankind from destruction and eternal separation from the Father.

Man fell in the Garden and lost his authority. Jesus came to redeem and restore that authority back to us here on the earth.

Genesis 1:26-28:

> "God said, Let Us [Father, Son, and Holy Spirit] make mankind in Our image, after Our likeness, and let them have complete authority over the fish of the sea, the birds of the air, the [tame]

beasts, and over all the earth, and over everything that creeps upon the earth. So God created man in His own image, in the image and likeness of God He created him; male and female He created them. And God blessed them and said to them, Be fruitful, multiply, and fill the earth, and subdue it [using all its vast resources in the service of God and man]; and have dominion over the fish of the sea, the birds of the air, and over every living creature that moves upon the earth."

God not only created man, but gave him complete control and authority over the whole earth.

Genesis 2:15-17:

"And the Lord God took the man, and put him in the Garden of Eden to tend and guard and keep it. And the Lord God commanded the man saying, You may freely eat of every tree of the garden; But of the tree of the knowledge of good and evil and blessing and calamity you shall not eat, for in the day that you eat of it you shall surely die."

God gave Adam a command that entailed what he was to do and what he was not to do. God gave Adam a Word.

Then the serpent came to the woman, Eve, and challenged her concerning the Word God had given to Adam.

Genesis 3:1:

> "Now the serpent was more subtle and crafty than any living creature of the field which the Lord God had made. And he [Satan] said to the woman, Can it really be that God has said, You shall not eat from every tree of the garden?"

Notice, that is not what God said.

Verses 2-3:

> "And the woman said to the serpent, We may eat the fruit from the trees of the garden, except the fruit from the tree which is in the middle of the garden. God has said, You shall not eat of it, neither shall you touch it, lest you die."

Again, notice God did *not* say they could not touch it. KNOW WHAT GOD SAID.

You may know the rest of the story—she and Adam did eat and were cast from the Garden of Eden, and man lost his authority here in the earth.

Adam was unprepared for the challenge. He allowed his faith to be moved; his faith in what God had said to him. God gave him a word, and he should have repeated that word to the devil when he came to attack.

Well, thank God for Jesus and His obedience to the Father and the Word. It is because of Jesus we get a second chance at living in the Kingdom.

Make a decision today to start fresh by spending time in the Word.

CHAPTER SEVEN

Act the Word

Have you ever gone to see a play, or musical, or even a movie? The actors act the part of the characters they play. They are given a script, which they memorize. Then they have to rehearse because they don't always get it right the first time. There's also a director who helps to put it all together, so that when the curtain goes up, the performance will be perfect.

Most Christians have a difficult time in this area of acting on the Word. However, Jesus not only demonstrated how to act the Word, He instructed us to act the Word.

In Mark 1:40-42, we read:

> "And a leper came to Him, begging Him on his knees and saying to Him, If You are willing, You are able to make me clean.
>
> And being moved with pity and sympathy, Jesus reached out His hand and touched him, and said to him, I am willing; be made clean!

And at once the leprosy [completely] left him and he was made clean [by being healed]."

Jesus was the Word in action.

Mark 2:2-5a, 11:

> "And so many people gathered together there that there was no longer room [for them], not even around the door; and He was discussing the Word.
>
> Then they came, bringing a paralytic to Him, who had been picked up and was being carried by four men. And when they could not get him to a place in front of Jesus because of the throng, they dug through the roof above Him; and when they had scooped out an opening, they let down the [thickly padded] quilt or mat upon which the paralyzed man lay.
>
> And when Jesus saw their faith [their confidence in God through Him]...."

(See how these men were acting the Word?)

> "....He said to the paralyzed man, Son, your sins are forgiven [you]."

Verse 11:

> "I say to you, arise, pick up and carry your sleeping pad or mat, and be going on home."

Joint heirs, this is very powerful. Remember, faith is acting the word; acting on what is written in scripture.

These men were willing to do whatever it took to gain access to Jesus. They were not moved by the fact that the natural circumstances said, "Go home. The man will just have to stay sick." The circumstances spoke out loud and said, "There's no room, not even outside the door."

Remember, they were carrying this man on a bed. The circumstances spoke and said, "Go away. You can't see Jesus today. No miracle today. No healing today. He can't meet your need today."

The circumstances spoke loudly and said "NO" to their miracle, but the men moved beyond the circumstances and acted the Word. I'm sure it was dangerous climbing on the roof with a crippled man. Sweat was probably running down their brows as they lifted their friend, being careful not to drop him. Don't forget that they also had to destroy someone else's property by tearing up the roof.

Then in Luke 5:4-7:

> "When He [Jesus] had stopped speaking, He said to Simon (Peter), Put out into the deep [water] and lower your nets for a haul.
>
> And Simon (Peter) answered, Master we toiled all night [exhaustingly] and caught nothing [in our nets]. But on the ground of Your word, I will lower the nets [again]. And when they had done this, they caught a great number of fish; and as their nets were [at the point of] breaking, they signaled to their partners in the other boat to come and take hold with them. And they came and filled both the boats, so that they began to sink."

What an amazing story! Peter and his company were fisherman. They knew all about fishing. Simon tells Jesus, "We have been out here all night, and there are no fish. But at your word, at your instructions, simply because You said so, I will let the net down again."

By doing as Jesus said, Peter caught so many fish that he needed help and the nets almost broke. Verse 7 says the boats began to sink because there were so many fish. Peter acted on the word he received from Jesus, even though the circumstances didn't agree with what Jesus said to do. Peter knew he had a word from Jesus, and that word was more powerful than the circumstances.

Luke 17:12-14:

> "And as He [Jesus] was going into one village, He
> was met by ten lepers, who stood at a distance.
> And they raised up their voices and called, Jesus,
> Master, take pity and have mercy on us!
>
> And when He saw them, He said to them Go [at
> once] and show yourselves to the priests. And as
> they went, they were cured and made clean."

Leprosy is a horrible disease that affects the skin, nerves, limbs and eyes. The disease causes permanent disability and disfigurement, and those afflicted were forced into quarantine, living in exile from the general public. This is what makes this incident powerful, as well.

When Jesus told the ten lepers to go and show themselves to the priests, nothing had changed for them. They still looked the same. They still had the same disfigurements. But they decided to act on what Jesus said, rather than focus on their current situation. According to the Law of Moses (Lev. 13:1-8) one was to be examined by the priest to determine if the disease was a detriment to others. Their obedience to start moving, in spite of not seeing any difference with the natural eye, is an amazing act of faith. The Bible says: "And as they went, they were cured and made clean."

How desperate are you for your situation to change? What lengths are you willing to go to trust God and receive an answer, or a miracle, or a need met? Ask yourself, "How can I act the Word today." Begin doing that now. Start with the small things, so that when the giant shows up you will be prepared.

Say the Word

Now that we have discussed the importance of *knowing* the Word, we have the foundation so we can properly *confess* the Word. Yes, speaking the Word, and speaking it out loud. This must be done daily and consistently. How long? Until Jesus returns. Why? Because He said so, and that makes it law.

Remember when Jesus spoke to the fig tree? He spoke out loud. How do we know? Because the disciples heard him.

In Luke 17:5, we see the disciples asking Jesus to increase their faith. Ever feel like you needed to have your faith increased? Sure you have. We all have.

So what do you think Jesus says in reply? "Sure, I'll just lay hands on you and increase your faith." Or, "Let's go to the garden and fast and pray. That will increase your faith." Or maybe, "Let's go to the synagogue and give a large sum of money. Surely this will increase your faith."

Luke 17:6:

> "And the Lord said, If ye had faith as a grain of mustard seed, ye might say unto this sycamine tree, Be thou plucked up by the root, and be thou planted in the sea; and it should obey you."
>
> (KJV)

Jesus immediately tells the disciples that their faith and what they say are tied together to produce all the faith they will ever need. He said that even if they had a small amount of faith, and would open their mouths and speak, it would cause to come to pass what they had commanded. The same is true for us.

This is *powerful.*

As you speak, you need to see the end result. You must look into the future and see the result of what you say. Jesus saw Himself victorious in what He came to do. We know this because He talked about His death and resurrection:

> "Hereafter shall the Son of man sit on the right hand of the power of God."
>
> (LUKE 22:69 KJV.)

> "Then said Jesus unto them, Yet a little while am I with you, then I go unto him that sent me."
>
> (JOHN 7:33 KJV.)

"The Spirit of the Lord [is] upon Me, because He has anointed Me [the Anointed One, the Messiah] to preach the good news (the Gospel) to the poor; He has sent Me to announce release to the captives and recovery of sight to the blind, to send forth as delivered those who are oppressed [who are downtrodden, bruised, crushed, and broken down by calamity], to proclaim the accepted and acceptable year of the Lord [the day when salvation and the free favors of God profusely abound]."

(LUKE 4:18-19.)

"Jesus said unto her, I am the resurrection, and the life: he that believeth in me, though he were dead, yet shall he live: And whosoever liveth and believeth in me shall never die. Believest thou this?"

(JOHN 11:25-26 KJV.)

When Jesus said these things, He had not yet gone to the cross. Even so, He spoke His victory long before it ever took place.

"Jesus replied, I am the Bread of Life. He who comes to Me will never be hungry, and he who believes in and cleaves to and trusts in and relies on Me will never thirst any more (at any time)."

(JOHN 6:35.)

"In My Father's house there are many dwelling places (homes). If it were not so, I would have told you; for I am going away to prepare a place for you. And when (if) I go and make ready a place for you, I will come back again and will take you to Myself, that where I am you may be also."

(JOHN 14:2-3.)

"And deliver Him over to the Gentiles to be mocked and whipped and crucified, and He will be raised [to life] on the third day."

(MATTHEW 20:19.)

"For he taught his disciples, and said unto them, The Son of man is delivered into the hands of men, and they shall kill him; and after that he is killed and shall rise the third day."

(MARK 9:31 KJV)

"And they shall mock him, and shall scourge him, and shall spit upon him, and shall kill him: and the third day he shall rise again."

(MARK 10:34 KVJ)

"And they shall scourge him, and put him to death: and the third day he shall rise again."

(LUKE 18:33 KJV)

I pray by now you are saying to yourself, "OK, OK! Enough! I get it!"

Well, do you? Do we?

We confess something for two days and then say, "This stuff doesn't work." Well, Jesus *never* stopped speaking the Word.

Yes, we know Jesus spoke to the fig tree, and the wind, and the sea. Yes, He commanded demons to come out, and they obeyed. Yes, He spoke to the dead, and they began to breathe again. But He also consistently spoke the Word and will of God for His own life, and continued to do so until the very end of His earthly ministry. All the things Jesus said about Himself were already written down; had already been prophesied. But, what does Jesus do? He gives voice to the written Word, speaking out loud what was going to happen in His ministry and what He was sent to accomplish.

It was so important to God that the Word continue to be spoken that He had it all written in a book so we could keep speaking it as well. Jesus continually opened His mouth and gave voice to the prophecies and written Word concerning His life and ministry. Today, we give voice to that same powerful Word and cause our circumstances to line up with what we say, just like Jesus did when He walked the earth.

Hopefully, knowing this will help you as much as it has helped me. Jesus never stopped speaking and calling those things that are not, as though they were. He had not yet been delivered up. He had not yet been beaten. He had not yet been spit on. Jesus had not yet gone to the cross, nor had He risen from the dead—but He spoke of it. So to everyone, including myself, who has said, "How long do I have to keep saying this about my situation?" Jesus has given us the example. We are to keep saying it until it comes to pass.

Jesus knew His assignment. He came here with an assignment and knew exactly what He had been sent here to do. He also knew exactly how it would be accomplished and how long it would take to achieve that goal. Jesus had a plan; He visualized that plan and then continually spoke the plan.

This is the same way Christians are to live their victorious lives. We are not to go through life stumbling blindly from one career to another. One job to another, and somehow God's going to work it all out. After studying the life of Jesus, it is clear that as we spend time in prayer—communicating and fellowshipping with the Father—God the Father will reveal, by the Holy Spirit, our individual roles in life and how we are to achieve and fulfill our assignments.

Begin speaking the perfect will of God for your life. If you are faithful, the Lord will reveal His perfect will to you.

You may find it helpful to take a course on journaling. Learning to journal will change your life. Habakkuk 2:2:

> "And the Lord answered me and said, Write the vision and engrave it so plainly upon tablets that everyone who passes may [be able to] read [it easily and quickly] as he hastens by."

Again, learn to develop your imagination to see the end result until the manifestation of your faith comes to pass.

Jesus always led by example. Just think how much easier our journey through life will be if, as we fellowship with the Father, He begins to unfold the mystery of the Kingdom as it applies to each of us individually. I'm sure that would be much better than the way most of us are living our daily lives.

Meditate on how Jesus knew the plan and purpose for His life from the beginning. Share that in your prayer time with the Lord, and ask Him to reveal His will in your life. Meditate quietly, and be sure to write down the things you receive during prayer each day. This is called journaling. For more information on journaling go to: www.cwgministries.org.

Know the Word and How it Applies to Your Situation

"And he answered and said unto them, Have ye not read...."

(Matthew 19:4 KJV)

"Jesus saith unto them, Did you never read in the scriptures...."

(Matthew 21:42 KJV)

"Jesus answered and said unto them, Ye do err, not knowing the scriptures, nor the power of God."

(Matthew 22:29 KJV)

Once again, my point in sharing these scriptures is to emphasize that Jesus knew what the Word had to say, and He used the scripture in response to challenges. So, when faced with challenges, what do we need to do? We need to use the scripture to answer back—holler or scream back at whatever is "talking" to you.

Not long ago, I was in the kitchen washing a few dishes, and the TV was on in another room. I'm not sure if it was a commercial or a video, but I could hear the chorus of a song playing, and the catchy, little tune caught my ear. It was a female singing, and all I could hear was: "I ain't no holler back girl, I ain't no holler back girl."

Now I don't know what the rest of the song was about, and I probably don't want to know, but I thought to myself, 'When it comes to the word of God, you had better be a holler back girl! You need to holler back at all those circumstances talking to you night and day, and you have to holler back at sickness, and lack, and fear, and confusion!'

According to what Jesus said and did, you don't have to just sit there and take it. You don't even have to get into a struggle. You only need to do what Jesus did and speak the Word back to Satan.

Religion tries to make it more complicated than it is. Jesus has fought the battle and won the war. He made the winning touchdown, the final homerun, the hole-in-one that brought about victory for mankind. You only need rise up and see yourself as the champion Jesus has made you to be. So the next time you are faced with a situation, and fear tries to attack, ask yourself, "Who moved my faith?" Trust me, the situation will speak back and identify itself.

Once you recognize the culprit, you can tell it to line up with the Word of God. No longer will you have to go looking for your faith and wondering where it has gone. No more insecurity. You've got it! You've got your faith—it's in your mouth and in your heart.

Paul writes this in Romans 10:8:

> "But what does it say? The Word (God's message in Christ) is near you, on your lips and in your heart; that is, the Word (the message, the basis and object) of faith which we preach."

Jesus gave voice to the scripture to create and change circumstances and events. You and I are to follow His example. He has given us the same ability and authority He had when He walked the earth. John 14:12:

> "I assure you, most solemnly I tell you, if anyone steadfastly believes in Me, he will himself be able to do the things that I do; and he will do even greater things than these, because I go to the Father."

Jesus clearly states that the very things He did on earth, we are to do also. Jesus used the creative power of words to create, change and radically affect those around Him.

You may be asking yourself, "How do I put this into action?"

Glad you asked that question. Following are some scriptures to begin confessing and renewing your mind. This may seem a little strange at first if you are not used to talking out loud when no one else is around. However, if you will be consistent, after 30 days it will become a habit. It will seem like you have been doing this all your life. As you search the Bible yourself, begin to find scriptures that apply to your situation.

Romans 12:2:

> "Do not be conformed to this world (this age), [fashioned after and adapted to its external, superficial customs], but be transformed (changed) by the [entire] renewal of your mind [by its new ideals and its new attitude], so that you may prove [for yourselves] what is the good and acceptable and perfect will of God, even the thing which is good and acceptable and perfect [in His sight for you]."

So put your crown back on your head, slip into your royal robe, rub the dust off your gold sandals, and polish your ring. Point your finger at that situation and give the command. Jesus said it will obey you. Rejoice as though it's already done. Rejoice as you envision the victory. Praise God with dancing and music, for this day deliverance has come to your house.

The Language of the Kingdom

Every Kingdom has a language, and in order to operate, move and function in that Kingdom, one must learn the language. If you were to go to Africa, you would need to speak the language there. If you were to travel to India, you would need to learn to speak the language and learn the customs of that nation. So it is with the Kingdom of God. There is a full language in this Kingdom, and failure to use the language properly will result in you being confused and misdirected in the same way you would if you were in a foreign country and could not speak the language of the land.

The following scriptures are to help you begin to learn the language in the Kingdom of God. Remember, you must learn the language of the Kingdom in order to function and operate in it properly. Failure to learn the language and get it down into your spirit will definitely cause your faith to be moved.

Healing

Lord, I thank you that according to Your word, Jesus died on the cross not only for my salvation but also for my healing. According to Isaiah 53:5, You were wounded for my transgressions, chastisement (needful to obtain) peace and well-being was upon you and with the stripes (that wounded) You I am healed and made whole.

Exodus 15:26—I thank you Lord because, according to Your Word, You are the Lord that heals.

Matthew 12:15—Jesus, You healed everyone that came to You for healing. Healing is my covenant right. Therefore, in the name of Jesus, my body is healed from the top of my head to the souls of my feet.

Mark 11:23-24—The Word of God says that I can have whatever I say, therefore in the name of Jesus I speak healing to my body right now. Every disease and germ that tries to attach itself to my body must die instantly the moment it touches me. No sickness and no disease is allowed to dwell in this body, in Jesus name.

Hebrews 8:6—I have a new covenant, which is established on better promises. Divine healing is a part of my new covenant; therefore, I walk free from sickness and disease, in Jesus' name.

Lack/Poverty/Finances

Lord, Your Word says in 2 Corinthians 8:9, that You were rich, yet You became poor that through Your poverty I might become rich.

According to Philippians 4:19, my God shall supply all my need according to His riches in Glory by Christ Jesus. Therefore, I come against any lack in my life right now. I am a citizen of the Kingdom of God and I have an abundant supply of all things.

I sow bountifully according to 2 Corinthians 9:6. Because I sow bountifully and generously, I reap bountifully and generously and with blessings.

I thank you Lord because I am a giver, and because I am a giver, men give back to me. They pour into my pouch and I overflow with plenty. (Luke 6:38)

Jesus came that I might have life and have it in abundance (to the full, till it overflows). (John 10:10.) Therefore, each and every day I walk in the abundant life Jesus came to provide for me.

There can be no lack in my life because, according to Philippians 4:19, my God shall supply all my need according to His riches in glory by Christ Jesus.

Peace

I make a decision to let the peace of God rule in my heart, and worry will be far from me. (Colossians 3:15.)

Jesus, You said in Your Word that You provided peace to me for each and every situation I come up against. I thank You, Lord, again for that peace. I receive it fresh and anew in my heart and soul, and I rest in You, Lord, no matter what the circumstances. I'll not allow fear in my life. (John 14:27.)

Courage

Jesus, You said in Your word that if I lived in You, and You lived in me, I could ask whatever I will and it would be done for me. Thank You, Lord, for giving me this confidence that I know whatever I ask, according to Your Word, it will be done. (John 15:7)

I have the strength for all things through Christ Who empowers me. I am prepared and can handle anything through Him. (Philippians 4:13.)

Thank You, Lord, that the weapons of my warfare are not physical, but mighty through You, for the overthrow and destruction of strongholds. I walk in victory over the devil every day of my life. (2 Corinthians 10:4.)

Ministry

Jesus, You said in Your Word that signs would follow the believer. I'm a believer; therefore, signs follow me. In Jesus' name I cast out demons, I speak with new tongues, if I accidentally pick up a serpent or drink any deadly thing, it will not hurt me. I lay hands on the sick and they get well. (Mark 16:17–18.)

Because I desire to obey Jesus, I go into the world and preach the gospel wherever I go, and the Lord works with me to confirm the Word with signs following. (Mark 16:15, 20.)

Lord, I thank You that, just like Joshua, I will be strong and courageous. I will not turn from it to the right-hand or to the left, that I may prosper where I go. Your Word will not depart out of my mouth. Yes, I will meditate on Your Word day and night, and do all that is written in it. I will deal wisely and I will have good success. I will be strong and I will not be afraid, for I know You are with me wherever I go. (Joshua 1:7-9.)

Salvation

Perhaps you have never really confessed out loud that Jesus is Lord and invited Him into your heart and life. This is the most important of all confessions. If you have never received Jesus as Lord of your life, say this simple prayer:

Father, I thank You for sending Jesus to die on the cross for mankind. I thank You for sending Your only Son, Jesus, to redeem my life from destruction and eternal separation from You. Jesus, come into my heart right now. I repent of my sin and turn now to You and make You Lord and Savior of my life. Thank You, Jesus, for saving me and coming into my life so that I may be born again. In Jesus name. Amen.

Begin saying these scriptures each day. Spend time in the Word on your own, searching the scriptures. You will find this to be a wonderful time of fellowship with the Lord as He begins to reveal more and more secrets of the Kingdom to you. But you must initiate the time with Him.

You will become stronger and stronger in the Word and grow spiritually daily until you are sharing and teaching someone else and bringing others into the Kingdom. That's what the Kingdom is all about.

"And the Lord kept adding [to their number] daily those who were being saved (from spiritual death)."

(ACTS 2:47.)

What Do I Do Now?

Rarely does a person take the time to read a book about a particular subject and not have a desire to do something more in that area.

When talking with Christians concerning what they are believing God for, I often find myself thinking, 'I wish I had a tape recorder.' If I did, I would play back every word so they could hear what they are saying. Of course, this is something we have all been guilty of doing, but since I am writing the book, I get to tell about you and what it is you are saying. Just think, if one is speaking of things contrary to the Word with someone they barely know, what must they be saying about their situation when they are behind closed doors, or to people with whom they are even more comfortable?

If this sounds harsh, try being sick, or broke, or depressed, or having some traumatic experience happen to you or a member of your family. That's really harsh. Jesus said we are to change all of that by using our faith. So if you are waiting for Jesus to change your situation, I've got really bad news for you. He's not going to do it for you! You must initiate any changes that you want to occur in your life. On the cross, Jesus, Himself, said, "It is finished." In other words, He was telling us: "My part is done. I'm giving you back your position and authority in the earth. Take it!"

Yes, I said I was closing, but open your Bible one more time and let's look at Joshua Chapter 1.

You know the story. Moses has died, and Joshua is about to take command and become the leader of the children of Israel. God begins to instruct Joshua on what he must do—notice, Joshua had to do something.

Joshua 1:5-9:

> "No man shall be able to stand before you all the days of your life. As I was with Moses, so I will be with you; I will not fail you or forsake you. Be strong (confident) and of good courage, for you shall cause this people to inherit the land which I swore to their fathers to give them...."

(Did you see how God told Joshua that he, Joshua, would cause the people to inherit the land?)

> "....Only you be strong and very courageous, that you may do according to all the law which Moses My servant commanded you. Turn not from it to the right hand or to the left, that you may prosper wherever you go.

This Book of the Law, shall not depart out of your mouth, but you shall meditate on it day and night that you may observe and do according to all that is written in it. For then you shall make your way prosperous, and then you shall deal wisely and have good success.

Have not I commanded you? Be strong, vigorous, and very courageous. Be not afraid, neither be dismayed, for the Lord your God is with you wherever you go."

From this passage of scripture, can you see how God had a role to play, and Joshua had a role to play. So stop crying and begging God to change your situation. You are wasting your time and God's time! If you will get a hold of the Word and do like Joshua, God will honor your efforts. He will honor your obedience. He will honor your faithfulness.

Just open your mouth and say it! Say what? The Word! Then see the salvation of the Lord and all His glory.

People generally have difficulty with saying, and doing, and acting the Word because in the natural it doesn't make sense. If no one else has told you, please let me be the first—it will never make sense to your natural mind when it comes to obeying the commandments of God. God speaks and operates through your spirit man, not your mind.

Did it make sense for those ten lepers to get up and start walking on their way before they saw a difference in their physical body? Did it make sense for Peter to let down the net after he had just finished fishing all night long? Did it make any sense at all for a group of men to climb on top of the roof of a house with a lame man on a stretcher and tear up the roof so they could get in the presence of Jesus?

Speaking of not making sense, there's the story in the book of 2 Chronicles about King Jehoshaphat. This account is one that is very important to study line by line and precept upon precept.

King Jehoshaphat was a great king. In fact, the scripture says that he had riches and honor in abundance. God blessed Jehoshaphat because he did not seek other gods, and God established the kingdom in his hand. I want you to get the picture of just how great and mighty he was. The scripture goes on to state that terror fell on all the other kingdoms, and no one made war against Jehoshaphat.

Well, you know the enemy is not going to let you have peace for so long. In chapter 20, several armies decide they are going to attack and go into battle against Jehoshaphat. The Bible tells us that these armies were a great multitude. (2 Chronicles 20:2.)

2 Chronicles 20:3: "Then Jehoshaphat feared...."

He feared, but he also sought the Lord and proclaimed a fast in all Judah.

Verse 5:

> "And Judah gathered together to ask help from the Lord."

Notice, the people obeyed the request of their leader. Nobody showed up with an attitude like "What are we doing this for? Why don't we just suit up and go to war and defend ourselves?"

In verse 6, Jehoshaphat stands in the midst of the people and begins to speak to God. First he tells God how great He is. (Notice he has not said one word about the big army that is coming against him. Neither has he mentioned how afraid he really is.)

> "And [Jehoshaphat] said, O Lord, God of our fathers, are You not God in heaven? And do You not rule over all the kingdoms of the nations? In Your hand are power and might, so that none is able to withstand You. Did not You, O our God, drive out the inhabitants of this land before Your people Israel and give it forever to the descendants of Abraham Your friend? They dwelt in it and have built You a sanctuary in it for Your Name saying, If evil comes upon us, the sword of judgment, or pestilence or famine, we will stand before this house and before You--for

> Your Name [and the symbol of Your presence]
> is in this house--and cry to You in our affliction,
> and You will hear and save."
>
> (2 CHRONICLES 20:6-9)

Jehoshaphat is reminding God that when He gave them the land, the men of Ammon, Moab and Mount Seir existed there, and Israel did not invade and drive them out. Jehoshaphat is now telling God they are coming to war against the Israelites and this is the thanks they get for allowing these people to stay. In other words, "Look how they are thanking us."

Verse 11:

> "Behold, they reward us by coming to drive us
> out of Your possession which You have given us
> to inherit."

Jehoshaphat then asks God to exercise judgment on them.

> "For we have no might to stand against this great
> company that is coming against us. We do not
> know what to do, but our eyes are upon You."
>
> (2 CHRONICLES 20:12B)

Remember back for a moment to the story of Joshua and Caleb, when the spies returned from the land of Canaan. Remember the negative report? Jehoshaphat and the people of Judah have quite a different attitude and confession. They are saying "Yea, there are more of them than there are of us, and we don't know what to do, BUT we are going to fix our eyes on You, and You are going to exercise judgment on these armies."

Verse 13:

> "And all Judah stood before the Lord, with their children and their wives."

GOD SHOWS UP TO HELP THEM.

Verses 14-15:

> "Then the Spirit of the Lord came upon Jahaziel son of Zechariah ... He said, Hearken, all Judah, you inhabitants of Jerusalem, and you King Jehoshaphat. The Lord says this to you: Be not afraid or dismayed at this great multitude; for the battle is not yours, but God's."

God not only shows up to help, but reveals the enemy's battle plans.

Verses 16-17:

> "Tomorrow go down to them. Behold, they will come up by the Ascent of Ziz, and you will find them at the end of the ravine before the Wilderness of Jeruel. You shall not need to fight in this battle; take your positions, stand still, and

see the deliverance of the Lord [Who is] with you, O Judah and Jerusalem. Fear not nor be dismayed. Tomorrow go out against them, for the Lord is with you."

Watch this:

Verses 18-19:

"And Jehoshaphat bowed his head with his face to the ground, and ALL Judah and the inhabitants of Jerusalem fell down before the Lord, worshiping Him. And some Levites of the Kohathites and Korahites stood up to praise the Lord, the God of Israel, with a very loud voice."

Verses 20-22:

"And they rose early in the morning and went out into the Wilderness of Tekoa; and as they went out, Jehoshaphat stood and said, Hear me, O Judah, and you inhabitants of Jerusalem! Believe in the Lord your God and you shall be established; believe and remain steadfast to His prophets and you shall prosper.

When he had consulted with the people, he appointed singers to sing to the Lord and praise Him in their holy [priestly] garments as they went out before the army, SAYING, Give thanks to the Lord, for His mercy and loving-kindness endure forever!

And when they began to sing and to praise, the Lord set ambushments against the men of Ammon, Moab, and Mount Seir who had come against Judah, and they were [self-] slaughtered."

The Word goes on to say that they all helped to destroy one another, and when the people came to collect the spoil, they found cattle, goods, garments, and precious things—more than they could carry away. It took them three whole days to gather it all.

This was clearly a situation that seemed impossible. None of Jehoshaphat's instructions made sense in the natural to any king or commander of an army, but he chose to follow God's instructions and he came out victorious.

Then there is another example to be found in the New Testament:

Matthew 9:20-22:

"And behold, a woman who had suffered from a flow of blood for twelve years came up behind Him and touched the fringe of His garment; For she kept SAYING to herself, If I only touch His garment, I shall be restored to health.

> Jesus turned around and, seeing her, He said,
> Take courage, daughter! Your faith has made
> you well. And at once the woman was restored
> to health."

According to Leviticus 15, this woman lived as an outcast, similar to that of the leper. She was considered unclean. Not only that, but according to verse 19, whoever touches her shall be unclean. She defied the law and sought after Jesus for her healing. She heard about the miracles and, based on what she heard, she knew He was the hope she had been waiting for these twelve long years. She was sick and broke and no doctor could help her, but she did not look at her situation. She focused on Jesus, pushed her way through the crowd, reached out and got her miracle.

Again, Jesus makes public mention about the demonstration of an individual's faith. He stops everything and wants to know who the one person was that had touched Him in the middle of an uncontrollable crowd. (Luke 8:45.)

"'Who touched me?' He asked."

Wouldn't you like to have Jesus say that about you the next time you have a need? I sure would. To have the Master take note and make mention of my faith in Him--what an awesome experience. Jesus giving public recognition for faith demonstrated concerning His Word. Faith must be recognizable. Faith must be demonstrated according to, and in line with, the Word of God.

This is the only prevention against having one's faith moved by the circumstances instead of demonstrating the mountain-moving faith Jesus said each of us possess.

It is my prayer that you have learned something new or been reminded of some topics you once had a handle on.

Growing up in Christ should be the ultimate goal for every believer. This is a process and a journey we will travel until Christ returns. In the meantime, we must work to establish the Kingdom and win as many souls as we possibly can. In order to do that we must not let anything, or any situation, move our faith from the foundation on which it was built— our Lord and Savior, Jesus Christ.

It's Sunday morning and the church is packed. As usual, the pastor is excited, and the congregation, INCLUDING YOU, is standing on their feet. This time, you shout, "I am more than a conqueror, and I will not be defeated!"